How to pick the right one

Five steps to pick an accountant that can

SAVE YOU TAX

Chantal Matthews FMAAT

Legal Notices and Disclaimer.

Forward

Let's face it, accounting and tax are not the most exciting topics for most of us. So, well done for opening this book and reading this far. Stick with it and you might even find it helpful.

I think we can all agree that the consequences of not addressing the basic tax regulations could be dire for our finances and potentially, our future life plans. It is a subject we all know we SHOULD understand and SHOULD keep up to date with, but who really does? Who has the time? I certainly don't and if I'm being honest, I'd rather do almost anything else instead!

My husband and I run a building firm and after years of using the same 'old school' accountant we realized that for us to grow the business we needed some serious financial planning and guidance. We just simply didn't know enough about taxes or accounting to be sure that we were being efficient.

We were introduced to Chantal by a mutual friend just after we had been badly let down by an accountant, who had promised us the world and promptly disappeared without having done anything for nearly a year. The accounts were in a mess and we were no closer to achieving our goals.

In hindsight what we should have done then was jump onboard with Chantal, but we didn't. We decided to go with another accountant who was offering to resolve our chaos for free! Brilliant!

Fast forward a year and not only had the bare minimum been done, but we still had no real clarity on our finances, and we received quite a large tax bill. That's when we moved our accounting and bookkeeping to Chantal. Immediately she reviewed our accounts for the previous year and discovered we were due a tax refund of over £4,000.

Wow!!

The accountancy firm she built from scratch took a holistic approach, looking not just at the company accounts, but at all areas of our lives, helping us to plan for our family's future. Our meetings often took place at the kitchen table over a cuppa on a Saturday morning.

Working with Chantal we came to realise very quickly that we don't need to keep up to date with HMRC, nor do we have to read every new regulation. That is what a good accountant should be doing for you.

Her passion for her clients to succeed is matched only by her own drive for success.

Chantal has mentored and inspired (some may say bullied!) us into thinking beyond the 9 to 5.

Her passion and energy are immense, as is her heart.

Louisa Johnson

Table of contents

Chapter 1

Uniquely qualified

I guess you are wondering what qualifies me to give you advice on how to pick your accountant. That's why I have taken the opportunity in this chapter to give you a brief outline of my history and experience.

One of my oldest memories is living in a caravan next to my grandparents' home on the family farm, watching my parents come home from a long day at work and build our family home brick by brick. I guess that's where my love of property began.

From a young age a strong work ethic was instilled in our family. I can still remember working part time in my Uncle's greengrocer from the age of 13 during my summer holidays to earn pocket money. The words of my parents still ring in my ears, "Nothing in life is free and money doesn't grow on trees."

I completed my South African A level equivalent in Accounting and Business Sciences in 1993 with the aim of studying to become a charted accountant through the open university while working.

What a joke! Nothing had prepared me for the commitment and dedication needed to complete a degree in this manner and I failed miserably during my first year. Subsequently, I gave up my studies and focused on my job.

I started in the motor industry early in 1994 as a vehicle administration clerk and stock controller and within a couple of years I had been promoted to assistant accountant then branch accountant followed by group accountant and at the peak of my career in the industry, aged 32, I was one of a handful of female dealer principals in the country.

In 2008 after a very traumatic life-threatening experience I made the bold decision to give up my career in the motor industry, sell everything I owned and emigrate to the UK with my two young children.

Reflecting, arriving during the recession with just enough money to keep the three of us fed and housed for six months was probably not the best action plan and finding employment was a challenge.

I was blessed when Gordon, a Jeweller in Birmingham, offered me a part-time job, flexible around my childcare needs as his PA and office administrator. Before long I had taken over the duties as his company's financial controller. Gordon also encouraged me to gain my AAT accreditation as an accounting technician. Thanks to my accounting experience I was able to fastrack my studies in two years. While working two jobs and with the added duties of a single parent. I don't know who was more excited at my graduation my mom or me.

"Thank you Gordon, for seeing the potential in me"

Shortly after obtaining my licence to practice I opened my own accounting practice with the aim of training up the next generation of accountants through apprenticeships while offering accounting services to small and micro business.

I had no idea what I was signing up for. My first real business! OMG!. I had managed other people's businesses, but this was a whole new kettle of fish.

Thanks to hard work, dedication and the loyalty of amazing clients the practice grew quickly and within five years had reached a level where I could take a breath and reflect.

I realised that although the practice was growing nicely I was not going to be able to retire anytime soon and now, well past the half way mark it was time for me to work a miracle. I would need to change the way I did things. I had to find a way of investing for my retirement tax efficiently.

It was during this time that I remembered what my father had always told me, "If you want to be truly

wealthy you needed to own land and property."
However, I didn't even own my own home and every
penny I had was tied up in the business, there was no
chance of me releasing these funds any time soon.

In 2018 thanks to some outside the box thinking when
my children and I were issued a Section 21 notice to
vacate our rental property, due to the death of our
landlord, we managed to buy our first home in the UK
using 0% credit cards to raise the deposit. It is now
fifteen months later. We have managed to pay off half
of credit card debit already and the balance is still on
0% for a further 18 months and my son owns his own
home.

This got me thinking. Are there other creative ways of
building a property portfolio? I decided to start
educating myself in property.

I invested in professional training that has not only
taught me about all the different possibilities within
property, which are endless, but the training has taken
me on a personal journey too. It has taught me to focus
on making the changes necessary in my life to achieve
my goals and be happy.

I am sure that many of you can relate when I say, "In
my working career happiness seemed ever elusive."
This was especially the case while running my

accounting practice. Although I had always been involved in accounts in one shape or form it was not where my passion lay and studying the constant tax law changes was a tedious chore. I dreaded waking up in the morning and going to the office. Life is just too damn short not to do something that makes you happy.

Recently, when my key member of staff whom I had trained over the past five years to run the business with me, informed me that she was going to start her family and didn't want to return to work after the birth of her child. It was time to make some difficult decisions. I could start again and retrain someone new to manage the practice or I could let it go.

It was heart-breaking to make the decision to sell my accounting practice but deep down I knew this was the right choice for me. Not only would my clients be looked after by an accountant with many more years' experience and accreditations than I had, it would also give me the opportunity to focus on my new venture into property and follow my dream of becoming a public speaker.

Fast forward ten months and I am now a fully trained, registered and regulated, compliant deal sourcer or as some would call it a property broker. "What is that?"

I hear you say. Well I go out and find property investment opportunities for my investors.

The best part of my new role is helping others build wealth.

Chapter 2

What are you looking for?

The best place to start when looking for a financial professional is with you and your business. You need a clear vision of what it is that you need assistance with. Make a list of all the areas you think are potential problem areas and use this when interviewing potential professionals.

Like doctors and solicitors, accountants, bookkeepers and tax advisors generally specialise in a chosen area. Due to the scope of regular changes in legislation it is near on impossible for a single accountant to competently cover a range of different industries. I would therefore suggest that you pick a professional that specialises or has experience in your industry. You wouldn't take your car to the auto electrician for tyres, would you?

The different levels and types of accountants are priced very differently so clarity could not only save you time but could save you money too.

Generally, the larger or more complex the business, the larger the list of professionals needed. Also, remember that in larger businesses there is usually a financial department which will take care of everything from bookkeeping to management accounting.

It is important that you monitor your business and realise when you get to this point.

Although there are many types of accountants and financial advisors. in my opinion, these are the four most commonly used in smaller businesses; bookkeeper, accountant, tax advisor and financial advisor.

Over the next few pages I will explain these roles in further detail.

Bookkeeper

A bookkeeper is someone that records the financial transactions of your business. Too many small business owners feel that they can do the bookkeeping themselves and save money this way.

Think of bookkeeping as the foundations of your house; everything else will get built on these foundations. All your financial records and business decisions are based on the information that is produced from your bookkeeping. As when your house has poor foundations it will have structural issues, so will your business have issues if your bookkeeping is not accurate and up to date.

The area that most bookkeepers make mistakes in are qualifying business expenses and the recording of VAT.

I would suggest that if you choose to do your own bookkeeping you ask either your accountant or an external bookkeeper to audit your work once a year to ensure accuracy.

The services of a good bookkeeper can range from £10 - £30 / hour depending on your location, their experience and accreditations. But the most important piece of advice I can impart is USE SOFTWARE!! This will save time and money.

Accountant

An accountant generally prepares your financial statements and tax returns with the information supplied by your bookkeeper and then submits them to Companies House and HMRC on your behalf.

Some accountants will complete the bookkeeping too, but they are generally more expensive and in my experience a good bookkeeper will do the bookkeeping better than an accountant.

As I mentioned earlier accountants generally have their preferred niche or industry that they are more knowledgeable in. For example, in my firm we used to focus on micro businesses and trades.

People always ask me is it better to have a certified or a chartered accountant. I say it depends on the person.

I have known certified accountants who are worth their weight in gold and then I have also known charted accountants that do not have a clue on how a business is run. It all depends on your list of potential problem areas.

The law does help you in making your choice between a charted or a certified accountant to the extent that a certified accountant cannot perform an audit. So, if your assets are worth more than £5.1 million, you have more than fifty employees or your turnover (total sales) is more than £10.2 million then you will have to use the services of a charted accountant.

Accountants can charge anything from £35 - £250 / hour depending on their level of experience, expertise and the type of services required.

Tax Advisor

A good tax advisor is essential. Do you ever wonder how companies like Amazon pay so little tax? It's because they have some of the world's best tax advisors. Have you ever heard the saying that a good accountant should save you more in tax than what their fees are? Well this is most definitely the case with a tax advisor.

Tax Advisors are accountants that dedicate their careers to finding ways to save their clients tax, within the constraints of the law.

However, this comes with a warning! If it sounds too good to be true, then it is most likely not legal or not true. And not all tax advisors are good advisors. A good tax advisor's fees will start at £250 / hour.

Financial Advisors

The role of a financial advisor is to work alongside your tax advisor to assist you make informed decisions around pensions, investments and retirement products.

It is their duty to inform you of your investment choices.

I would recommend that you call a meeting with both your tax and financial advisors present at least once every five years to review your financial position and ensure you are still making tax efficient investments and planning for your future.

When choosing your financial advisor there are different types. There is an IFA (Independent Financial Advisor) they usually have access to a range of different investment opportunities from different providers and there is a FA (Finance Advisor). A FA is usually tied to one investment company instead of the whole of the market.

The price for a financial advisor can vary dramatically but remember there is no such thing as free. If your IFA does not charge you they will be earning a commission or fee from your investments.

Here's a news flash for you. Did you know, that even if you have an accountant and or a bookkeeper and if they get it wrong by submitting false or incorrect information to HMRC and companies house, you are still held responsible as the director of the company?

When looking for a competent, compliant professionals I would recommend that you look for those with accreditations, and recommendations. The letters behind their name have meaning and will give you an indication of their level of qualification and in some instances their chosen field. My letters FMAAT mean that I have been a member in practice of the AAT for five years.

I can hear you saying, "Well that doesn't help me much. How do I find the right accountant?" As I said earlier in this chapter you need to know what services you need before you start looking. Once you know what you are looking for then finding the right professional is so much easier.

Your first step is to tell as many people as you can that you are looking for an accountant. Every Tom, Dick and Harry will have someone to recommend. Make a list of these recommended professionals to start from.

Step two is to phone the professionals on your list and give them the:

Ten-question quiz.

1. Are you a bookkeeper, accountant or a tax advisor?
    - *As noted previously it is important to get the right person for the right job.*

2. Are you licensed and regulated and by which body?
    – This would apply to your bookkeeper too. They could have qualified 20 years ago and never updated their knowledge since. We all know how regularly government make tax changes so 20-year-old knowledge is no good to you.
    Once you have their accreditations check their regulatory body to ensure their license is up to date.

3. Who are your perfect/preferred clients?

– Listen carefully to their answer here because if they are not passionate about your type of business, they will not offer you the best service.

4. Do you require your clients to use a specific software?
– In 2019 we saw the arrival of MTD (Making Tax Digital). It's HMRC's plan to roll out MTD to all other forms of taxes in the future. This is why, it is imperative that business owners get used to using software to keep their records digitally. Software like Quickbooks & Xero are fantastic time savers and can help you manage your business and finances better. Most accountants have their preferred or chosen partners when it comes to software, pick the accountant that uses the same software as you do that way they will be able to assist you when you get stuck.

5. How regularly will we have meetings?
– So many times, I have sat in a meeting with a new potential client and I would ask the question, so why are you looking for a new accountant? Nine times out of ten the answer would be because I never hear from or see my current accountant unless they are asking for

*money. Communication is key. Many
accountants will promise you open lines of
communication during the initial meeting and
then change their mind down the line. I would
suggest you ask for their communication policy
in writing. You will want a minimum of one face
to face meeting with them annually and
unlimited email support.*

6. Going forward will I be dealing with you or a
   junior?
   *– The higher in the ranks within the practice,
   the more expensive. This is why clients usually
   get fobbed off onto a junior in the practice and
   only see the boss when there is a problem.
   Insist on a meeting with a senior partner once a
   year also insist that the junior who is your point
   of contact attends these meetings and is aware
   of what is been discussed. I would also suggest
   insisting that the work completed by the junior
   is signed off by a senior within the practice on a
   minimum of a quarterly basis.*

7. What are your fees and what do they cover?
   *– I cannot tell you how important it is to get
   clarification on what the fees cover upfront.
   When they say a monthly all inclusive, what is*

included? In so many cases I have seen clients sign a letter of engagement and pay monthly for services, they never received.

8. Is there a fixed monthly payment option?
   – In this day and age, we all need to haggle, many accounting firms will offer you a discount if you pay on account monthly. This is because not only can they confirm your continued custom in this way, but they can manage their cashflow better and are less likely to suffer bad debts. Remember you are benefiting them by paying monthly in advance and should therefore reap some sort of reward for this loyalty, hence insist on the discount.

9. Do you have any testimonials?
   – Don't be afraid to ask for testimonials and follow up these letters of reference with a phone call or a message to the author. In some cases, the testimonial could be years old and the level of service within the practice has depleted since then.

10. How many HMRC investigations do you deal with in a year?

– This question will give you an indication on the type of clients the accountant has. If they have more than one investigation a year proceed with caution. I know of a business that was pulled for three separate tax investigations all because their accountant was known by HMRC to represent clients with questionable ethics.

What next?

Those potentials that passed the quiz now go onto your shortlist and it is these professionals that you should book an appointment to go and see. If they are the right fit for your business, you will know once you meet them.

Many of my clients used to laugh at me but I would say, in the initial meeting "If you don't like me please don't choose my practice to work with you. We are going to have to work very closely in the coming years and you need to know, like and trust me for this to work."

Remember these are professionals trained to provide a service, a service that you are paying a lot of money for. So, insist on the highest level of said service.

Top Tip:

Know what you need before you start looking. Then book at least three, preferably five, meetings with potential candidates who have come recommended and passed the 10-question quiz.

Chapter 3

The importance of communication

Two of my favourite quotes about words:

C.S Lewis
"Don't use words too big for the subject. Don't say "infinitely" when you mean "very"; otherwise you'll have no word left when you want to talk about something really infinite."

Joseph Devlin
"To use a big word or a foreign word when a small one and a familiar one will answer the same purpose, is a sign of ignorance. Great speakers use simple words"

I am sure we have all been in the situation where we are sitting in a meeting with a professional and they use jargon and complex phrases that flummox you into submission.

My advice here is do not be afraid to question or appear ill-advised. We are all way too concerned in life about what others may think. I will let you in on a secret, what others think of you does not matter, it is what you think of yourself that counts.

In my opinion if a professional cannot explain something in an understandable manner then they are the foolish ones. Stand up for yourself and speak up. If you do not understand say so because no one is a mind reader.

So, when next they start rambling on about acid ratios and factoring, or anything else that you may not be familiar with, stop them. When you do not understand, get them to explain it to you so that you can understand. Most of the time they will not realise they are using terms you are unfamiliar with.

Let's look at an example shall we.

Bev takes her vehicle for a service to her local garage. A few hours later the service advisor phones Bev and says that the bushes on the tie rod ends are worn and need replacing. Bev instinctively asks how much this will cost to have it repaired? Bev then makes a decision based on how much it will cost.

However, if Bev asked the correct questions, "What is a tie rod end?" and "Why does it need to be repaired?" before she asked for the cost, she would know that it is an essential part of the steering system on her vehicle and the wear is due to the age of her vehicle and the bumpy farm road she travels to see her client every week.

This means that by asking the right questions Bev now knows that she does not have a choice, the repair needs to happen. More importantly she knows that her client will either need to pay her more for their weekly visits or will have to come to her for meetings.

The next key to good communication with your accountant is honesty. Don't be embarrassed or try and hide information from them. The more information you give them the better they will be able to help you. Knowledge is power!

A few years ago, I signed up a client and in the initial meeting the client informed me that their bookkeeping was not the best and they were concerned about their tax bill. What the client did not tell me was they were drawing down large amounts from the company to pay for their lifestyle. They also failed to share that their partner was unemployed but did help them with the company's administration.

It took my firm six months to clean up the bookkeeping and bring all the accounts up to date and find out the information above which the client had not told us during our meeting.

That six-month delay and omission of information cost the client an extra £10,601 in tax. If we had known about his lifestyle and partner in the beginning, we could have set up measures to avert the unnecessary tax.

During my time as an accountant I never attended a client meeting without an agenda or a list of topics that needed to be covered during the meeting.

Do the same when you attend a meeting. Make a list of questions and topics you want clarity on. This will not only ensure that you walk away with answers to your questions, but it will give the impression that you too are a professional who is to be taken seriously.

Top Tips:

Be honest and question everything, make sure you understand and be prepared for your meetings.

Chapter 4

Be prepared

I was a Brownie and a Girl Guide and live my life by their motto "Be Prepared"

During my time as an accountant it always shocked me how many people would come to the first meeting with me unprepared. They would not have any of their financial information with them but what shocked me the most is when I asked the question, "Do you have a business plan?" most would answer, "No." Those that did answer yes would say, "I did one a few years ago. I think it is in a file somewhere".

How do you expect the professional to take you seriously if you do not take your business seriously?

In the words of *Sir Winston Churchill*,

"He who fails to plan is planning to fail."

In this chapter I will briefly cover the importance of a business plan and give you a list of information you should have ready to take with you to your meeting.

I could go into detail about the importance of planning and the mechanics of it all but that is another book in itself.

The dreaded business plan. Why is it that so many of us look at a business plan as an arduous chore?

The most common excuses I hear are; "I don't know how," or "I don't have the time."

The problem is people's perception of a business plan. What do you picture when I say business plan? Is it a professional looking ring bound document? Good news, this does not have to be the case. There are different types of business plans for different situations.

For example, if you are approaching a bank for a loan to buy a new piece of machinery. You would want a plan that services that purpose, one that looks professional and covers all the key information required for the bank to make a decision.

However, in my opinion the most important business plan is the two- or three-page document that you keep in sight daily. You use it as a tool to review and score your progress every week.

Think of it this way, you would not go on a holiday without planning your journey, packing your suitcase and making your travel arrangements. Well running a business is the same. If you amble along blindly you will get lost down a side-track along the way.

Having a plan even a simple one will keep you on track and help you achieve your goals.

I would suggest starting with a simple 2-page plan and review and score your progress every week. Use your plan to generate an action plan or a job list that you keep on your desk and refer to it daily.

In this plan you will cover the following headings:

1. Where you are now – *A brief outline of your business and its KPI (Key performance indicators)*
2. Where you want to be – *What are the goals you want to achieve over the next three months.*
3. How to get there – *What will you need to do or implement to achieve the goals above.*
4. SWOT analysis – *Split the page into 4 quadrants and list your strengths, weaknesses, opportunities and threats.*

At the end of the three-month period compare your financial information with the previous three month period. Review your weekly scores on from your job list. Revise your plan. Rinse and repeat!

Like I mentioned above there are different types of business plans for different situations and you would not use your 2 page wonder plan to tender for a contract but the 2 page wonder will help you monitor and manage your business more effectively.

You will be surprised by what you can accomplish when you plan to do so, and you action your plan.

When you meet with your potential accountant for the first time there is some key information you will need to take with you. It is always a good idea to have a list of questions to ask while you are there.

I have always found it useful, when I know I have an important meeting coming up, to keep a writing pad close to hand. When questions pop into my mind I write them down. These notes are then used to generate my list or my agenda for my meeting. There is nothing worse than walking out of a meeting getting to the car and thinking, "Oh damn I forgot to ask ……"

Here is a list of some of the questions I used to ask potential clients during the initial meeting. This might help you prepare for your meeting with a potential accountant.

- Under what structure do you trade / invest, a sole trader or limited company, trust etc.?
- What do you do / what are ALL your sources of income?
- What is the name of your company?

- What are your trading and registered addresses?
- Are you married?
- Do you have children?
- Why are you looking for a new accountant?
- How do you keep your records?
- What software packages do you use?
- Are your records up to date?
- What services do you require?
- Do you have a business plan?
- Do you have a bookkeeper?
- Do you use the services of any other financial professionals?
- Do you have your last financial statements or tax return with you?
- How much do you currently pay your accountant?
- Have you ever had a HMRC investigation?
- How do you fund growth in your business?
- Do you run a payroll?
- Do you have a pension plan in place?
- Are you VAT registered?
- Are you CIS registered?
- Do you run company vehicles?

Each of the above questions would then lead to further questions within that topic dependant on the answers.

What I would suggest is if your potential accountant does not ask similar questions then move onto the next candidate.

Information to take along to your meeting. The type of information is very dependent on the structure of your business.

As the most popular business structure is a Limited Company, I have listed below the information that your accountant may require for a Limited Company.

Side note: before I move on, I would like to remind you that accountants are not only regulated by specific accounting bodies but also by the ICO, and HMRC. They are required by law to comply with Anti money Laundering (AML) regulations and therefore some of documentation that they request from you is required by law.

Documents and information to take with you:

- Proof of ID
- Proof of address, not older than three months
- Proof of company registration
- Details of all shareholders and directors of the company
- If possible, an organisational chart of the company
- Accounting period end date (Fiscal year end)
- PAYE reference number
- PAYE accounts office reference number
- Company UTR (Unique tax reference number)
- Director & shareholder's UTR
- VAT registration details
- Companies House web filing code
- Date your company was registered
- Previous accountant's details
- Last financial statements and tax returns
- Business plan

And most importantly don't forget your list of questions for your potential new accountant.

Top Tip:

If you are prepared and have all your paperwork ready you are the one in control.

Chapter 5

You don't always get what you pay for.

When it came to me finding a buyer for my practice, I was devastated to be told that I was under charging my clients by more than 30%.

I knew that I had added a lot of value to my clients but had no idea how generous I had been. "You can't know what you don't know" *Jonathan Raymond.*

Reflecting, there were several elements that would have contributed to this. Namely; low self-confidence, trying to win new business, lack of experience and a passion to help others.

But this is not the case with most accounting practices. The majority charge a lot of money for what they do, so how do you know if you are getting the best value for money?

Ask for it!

Warning!! you can only ask for that which you know you want/need. If this warning puzzles you, go back to chapter 2.

Here are the 3 Magic steps to getting the best value.

Step 1 – Establish your list of needs and wants. Let's look at an example.

Meet Joe. He runs a barbershop. After hours on his feet all day the last thing he wants to do is come home to paperwork. Joe also inherited his grandma's house when she passed which he now rents out for a little extra income. Joe has no pension in place for his retirement one day and knows that this is something that needs to be addressed. Joe's business is a Limited Company and his financial statements are due to HMRC and companies house once a year.

Looking at Joe's situation this would be what he needs:

Bookkeeper – to systemise and automate the data collection of his business and reconcile his accounts. After the systems are in place Joe would have contact with his bookkeeper once a month.

Accountant – the accountant will take the information from the bookkeeper and complete the financial statements and tax returns and company secretarial duties. Joe should meet with his accountant twice a year. Once, a few months before his fiscal year end and again after the year-end to sign off the completed accounts and returns.

Tax Advisor – as Joe already has an investment property and runs a successful business, he would benefit from meeting with a tax advisor once a year to ensure that he is structured in the most tax efficient way.

Financial advisor & property specialist – because Joe has an investment property it would be beneficial for him to use the services of a financial advisor who understands property and how to grow a portfolio but who can also help him invest in a pension. Joe only needs to see his financial advisor once every 2-5 years.

Joe also knows that he is rubbish at remembering deadlines and dates. So, the professionals he chooses must add value by sending reminders, notifications and hold information events. But the most important factor of all is all the professionals he chooses must communicate with each other.

Step 2 – Communication & information gathering

Joe now needs to ensure that he can find the best value for money professionals who will also communicate with each other to ensure his best interests are at the forefront of all financial decisions.

His first port of call would be to ask for recommendations. Social media is great for this as everyone has an opinion. Joe pops a post on Facebook asking for recommendations. He is inundated with a long list of professionals. Joe notices that one name is mentioned a few times and his mate Rob the plumber has recommended ABC Financial services. Already he feels that ABC might be the right professionals for him, but Joe decides to continue Step 2 to the end.

Next Joe makes a list of the three most recommended professionals and does some digging. He reads their reviews on all social media platforms. Visits their websites and checks their endorsements on LinkedIn. We are in a digital age, and Joe uses this to his advantage. After completing his due diligence on the professionals, he phones them. He uses the 10 question quiz to create his shortlist and books a few appointments. Most accounting and financial professionals will have an initial meeting free of charge.

Joe uses what he learnt in Chapters 3&4 to be prepared for his meeting. He has an agenda, a list of requirements and most importantly he is going to be honest and transparent. Joe knows that he is an ostrich when it comes to his finances and would much rather put his head in the sand than deal with budgets and bank accounts. He also has the tendency to lose purchase receipts and documents. Joe knows that the more information he can give them up front the more realistic their quote will be.

When the meeting is drawing to an end, Joe askes for an email covering what was discussed in the meeting. Especially relating to topics around expectation on time frames and pricing for services required.

Step 3 – Make an informed decision.

After receiving the emails and meeting with the potential professionals Joe can now see that ABC Financial services would not be the best option for him. They are focused more around very small business and sole traders, they did not have a tax advisor and did not work closely with any financial advisors.

After reviewing his top three Joe has decided to engage XYZ Accounts & More to help him with his list of requirements. Joe's wife Mandy is not very happy with his decision as she feels that XYZ are expensive. Joe explains to Mandy the process he went through to ensure he gets the best value for money. He also reassures her that after a year, if they do not offer the services agreed at the expected level, then they could always change to a different accountant.

As you can see there are no quick fixes or snap decisions when looking for value for money.

In my opinion many of us settle for second best because we are too lazy to look for better.

In some cases, we are penny wise and pound foolish. I look at it this way, I can cut my son's hair myself and did so for years. He saves £10 by letting me cut his hair. It takes me two hours to cut his hair. My hourly rate starts at £65/hour so in fact my son's hair cut costs me £130. Needless to say, he now goes to the barber.

The Top Tips:

If you want something, ask for it. If you can't afford what you are asking for, then ask yourself, "How can I earn the money to afford what I need?" Never settle because you are in a comfort zone. Speak up! If you feel like you are not getting what you are paying for say something.

Chapter 6

What should you be doing?

I was visiting a friend this week who owns his own MOT and Service Centre. While having a chat he asked me to help him track down an issue on a part they had ordered from a supplier that had failed. Within minutes we had all the information and while getting that information we also noticed that he would need to register for VAT soon and that was going to change a few things in his business.

He was astounded to see how quickly this information and a resolution was achieved. I said to him, "The numbers don't lie. If you understand how to read the numbers and know where to look for the problems and as long as your bookkeeping is accurate and up to date you will find what you looking for."

This is why, I think the most IMPORTANT duty you have to yourself and your business is understanding your numbers.

It is your duty to ensure your accountant helps you understand the numbers.

The biggest problem I see in business is that the person signing the financials and tax returns has no idea of what they are signing. The financials are not explained to them in detail. Items like KPIs (Key Performance Indicators) have not been discussed and there is no added value. If you do not understand your financial situation, how do you expect to improve it?

Why is it that as grownups we are so scared of asking questions? As children we all had enquiring minds and wanted to know why and how. But as we approached adulthood and navigated through the "know it all" teenager years, we seem to have forgotten this key skill in life, an inquiring mind. Is it that we are afraid of appearing stupid? Bruce Lee once said, "An intelligent mind is an inquiring mind."

When next you sit down to sign your accounts with your accountant get them to explain the financials to you page by page in layman's terms. Ask them questions as they go. Questions like; "Is that a normal profit margin for my industry? Why are my expenses so much higher this year than last?" This process has many advantages. It will help you understand your accounts better and that will help manage your business better. It will also identify any errors that may have occurred while preparing your accounts. Accountants, contrary to popular belief are only humans and make mistakes too.

Your next step would be to play to your strengths. Systemise and automate as much as you can.

Only spend your time on the important tasks like making the money and growing your business. Nobody goes into business not to make money. That is a charity not a business. Work on your business not in your business.

If like Joe you have 'financial phobia' then systemising will give you more control and comfort knowing it is all in hand.

Thanks to the digital age systemisation has never been easier. There are apps and software solutions for almost every problem you might face. And if learning how to use tech frightens you more than your accounts and finances do, then outsource.

The world has become incredibly small over the past few decades. I remember as a child writing letters to my aunt in New Zealand and waiting months to receive her postal reply. Now it's all instant messaging, emails and social media. We also tend to forget how powerful the Great British Pound Sterling is. Did you know, you could hire yourself a virtual assistant from the Philippines for as little as £200 a month for 40 hours a week?

But be warned to systemise and outsource your business you need to know your business inside out. That means having instructional videos and/or written instructions on how each task is performed from beginning to end. The more detailed these instructions are the better your Minions can serve you. Not only that, but if your instructions are recorded in this manner when you hire or look for new solutions you won't have to repeat or retrain and this could save you hours if not days.

In my accounting business I chose to employ apprentices and by the time we had employed the 3rd and 4th my involvement in their training had been reduced from 20 hours a week to just 2. This was only possible because every task had detailed instructions. I was there to resolve any complicated issued they may have encountered.

Let's look at Joe's business again. After engaging XYZ Accounts & More, Joe was allocated Jane, the practice bookkeeper, to help him systemise his business for higher efficiency. Jane put Joe's books onto Xero software and linked his bank accounts and card payment machine to the software. Jane also helped Joe write to all his suppliers and all receipts and purchase invoices are now emailed directly into the Xero software. Jane loaded the Xero app onto Joe's phone and showed him how to take a photo of a receipt and upload it to the software, ready for Jane to process. Now, the bookkeeping that used to take Joe an hour each night, takes Jane half an hour each week to do. This time saving alone has paid for Jane's portion of the accounting fees. But that's not all. Jane also put Joe in touch with a social media consultant, Jack. Joe's business has now increased revenue by 30% thanks to the Facebook marketing campaign and booking system Jack set up for Joe on Facebook.

The benefits of a good accountant don't stop there. When Joe engaged the services of XYZ Accounts & More he was offered a consultation with their tax advisor and financial advisor. Joe and his advisors decided to move his grandma's house into a company structure, finance the property and use the funds raised to grow Joe's property portfolio. Joe's property company now generates enough income for him and his wife to retire whenever they want.

The best part is that although XYZ Accounts & More, cost Joe double of what his previous accountant did. The savings in time and tax achieved cover the accounting costs in full each year and with the growth in revenue Joe now has a manager running the business which affords him the freedom to spend more time with his family.

So, what do you need to do?

TAKE ACTION!!! Get off your butt and find the right solutions for your business.

When I arrived in the UK eleven years ago I was astounded to find how outdated business practices were in general. For example, one of the business I worked for shortly after arrival, still issued handwritten receipts to its customers.

There are so many apps and solutions out there to make you more efficient and many of them are easy to use. Most of them will have a free trial period too. These apps and tools have been developed to help businesses systemise and automate functions to increase productivity and efficiency. So why are you not using them? Some of the business owners I chat to say they don't use them because of cost. But have they evaluated the financial benefits of the time saved?

Where do you find these solutions? Although an accountant will be a good source for automated solutions their experience might be limited to financial solutions. In my experience the best place to find out about these systemisation tools is to attend trade fairs and seminars relevant to your industry. When attending these fairs and seminars speak to likeminded people in your industry. You will find that most of us have the same problems and sharing solutions helps us all achieve more.

It goes back to what I said in the previous chapter, "Don't be afraid to ask."

I am reminded of when I started my accounting practice five years ago. I had no experience at all in how to run a practice never mind how to do this efficiently. I went to local networking events and tried to speak to other accounting professionals and ask for help. One thing I can say about the accounting profession is that it is extremely competitive, and no one wanted to help a newbie. In their opinion there was enough competition in the marketplace already.

This changed when I started attending the annual accounting conference and seminar in London. Here I was surrounded by thousands of accountants all looking for knowledge on how to do their job more efficiently.

There were hundreds of different automation solutions, seminars and how-to demonstrations. After attending my first Accountex in 2016 I implemented many of the systems I had learnt about. In 2017 my turnover increased by 61% and my bottom line improved by 72%. I am sure you can now see the value in attending a tradeshow relevant to your industry.

Top Tips:

When performing your daily tasks think, "Which of those tasks can be outsourced or automated and make a list." Once you have this list record a how-to manual and outsource. If you outsource ensure that you perform regular checks and have controls in place to make sure the work is done to your standard.

Be intelligent and ask many questions, don't stop asking until you understand.

Chapter 7

Still need help?

I know all too well what it is like reading a book like this and thinking, "Well that's alright for some but how do I action this? I just can't do it!"

I need someone to hold my hand, to make me accountable, someone to interpret the gibberish.

Well I've got you covered there. Over the next few pages I have created a glossary of the gibberish. I explain the basics of bookkeeping and at the end of the book are contact details where you can get in touch if you need any extra help.

Here is a recap of your five steps:

Step 1 – Spread the word, tell as many people as you can that you are looking for a new accountant and ask for referrals.

Step 2 – Know what you need. Have a clear understanding of the professional services you need.

Step 3 – Phone all potentials and give them the 10-question quiz. Create your shortlist to book a minimum of 3 face to face meetings.

Step 4 – Be prepared. Have your financial information, documents and business plan ready to take with you to the meeting.

Step 5 – Communicate, understand and negotiate

If there is one thing you remember or takeaway from the next few pages, it should be that bookkeeping & accounting is a double entry system. That means it works almost like a balancing scale

Every transaction in your business will have two parts. For every debit there will be a credit. Or, for every positive there will be a negative, herein retaining the balance.

Think of it this way. You buy a new pickup for the business. Your bank account will decrease but your fixed assets will increase. In accounting terms, you will credit your bank account and debit your fixed assets account.

I am sure you have heard terms like your accounts don't balance. That is because there is an error in your bookkeeping. With the aid of software this is a lot less relevant. The software does most of the double entry for you.

All you need to do is make sure you are processing the correct transactions to the correct accounts using the correct source documentation.

This is how your accounts are produced in a very brief summary.

TRANSACTIONS. These are purchases and sales etc.

↓

LEDGERS. Your transactions are recorded in your general, purchase and sales ledger.

↓

TRIAL BALANCE (TB). The balances in your ledgers are carried over to your trial balance. Your trial balance is used to check the accuracy of your ledgers.

↓

P&L (Profit and Loss) statement. The account totals from the extended trial balance are then carried across either to the P&L or the BS. The Profit and loss statement will report your profit in the business.

↓

BALANCE SHEET(Statement of financial position/BS) The BS account totals from the TB are then recorded and summarised in your balance sheet along with the profit which has been carried over from your P&L statement.

Jargon buster

AAT – Association of Accounting Technicians is a professional body that trains and licenses accountants to practise these will be certified but not charted accountants. An accountant that is AAT registered will have the AAT letters after their name and will be expected to maintain high levels of CPD (Continued Professional Development)

ACCA – Association of Chartered Certified Accountants. This a world recognised accounting body that supports charted accountants. If your accountant is a member of the ACCA they will have the letters ACCA behind their name. They might have FCCA and that means that they are a fellow member and have been a member for a minimum of five years.

AE - Accrued Expenses are expenses that relate to the period that you are reporting on but have not been paid yet. E.g. Corporation Tax.

AP - Accounts Payable - also known as creditors. This is the amount of money your company owes its creditors. Creditors are those that supply your company on payment terms. Your accounts payable are recorded in your balance sheet in the current asset section.

AR - Accounts Receivable or also known as debtors. Debtors are those that owe you money. They would be recorded in your current assets of your balance sheet and should be managed carefully to mitigate losses.

ATT – Association of Taxation Technicians is a professional body assisting those providing tax compliance services and related activities. Like all the other accounting bodies the highest level of CPD is require to retain your membership and a qualified member will have the letters ATT after their name.

B2B – Business 2 Business. This acronym is commonly used on grant applications and means that your customers are another business. An example of this would be an accounting firm whose business is serving other businesses.

B2C – Business 2 Customer. This means that your clients or customers are the end users and are individuals and not companies. An example of a B2C business would be a barber.

BS – NO! this does not stand for bull shit. It means Balance Sheet. Your balance sheet, also referred to as your statement of financial position, is a snapshot of your business's financial standing on a particular date. It summarises your assets less your liabilities and your shareholders equity.

BV - Business Valuation like any valuation is not what the business is worth. The business is only worth what someone else is willing to pay you for it. There are different matrix used to value business and the one used for your business will depend on your industry.

CA – Current Assets are assets that can be converted into cash within one year. Examples of current assets are; inventory, debtors and bank accounts (if the bank account is in a positive balance). A CA could also mean a Charted Accountant.

CAP – Capital is the value of a financial asset. Sometimes you will hear reference to working capital. This is calculated by subtracting your current assets from your current liabilities. The result is the amount of money available to your company to put to work.

CF – Cash Flow. In my opinion this is the most important and usually the most neglected part of any business. This measures the movement of money in and out of your business and is the main tool I use in budgets and forecasts.

CIMA – Charted Institute of Management Accountants is the accounting body which supports and trains management accountants for industry and business. You would find a management accountant in larger business and they would take control of the internal accounting function of the business.

CIOT – Chartered Institute of Taxation is a charity and professional body that supports its members solely in taxation. This is arguably the qualification that carries the most punch. We all would like to reduce our tax bill and CIOT members are the ones that can help us achieve this.

COS - Cost of Goods Sold. There are many ways of calculating your COS and the way used will depend on your industry. The COS is usually split into direct and indirect costs. Direct costs would be items used directly in the production of your products, for example the cream in ice cream. An indirect cost is one that you could do without or that is not a necessity, for example the receptionist.

CL – Current Liability is an amount owed by your company to a creditor and is payable within a year. Examples of current liabilities are bank over drafts and suppliers that offer goods/services on credit.

CPD – Continued Professional Development is a requirement by all accounting professional bodies. It ensures that members update their knowledge of the sector on a regular basis. In my case I used to spend twenty hours a week on my CPD.

CPU - Cost Per Unit is measured using a cost card. This is a detailed report of all the costs involved in producing one unit of your product.

CR - Credit. In accounting a credit is the name we give to a transaction that will decrease your assets and increase your liabilities.

CT – Corporation Tax is the amount of tax your business will pay on its profits. Always ensure that your accountant is aware of tax allowances such as Capital Allowances and R&D tax reliefs. These could save you a lot of tax.

DR - Debit. In accounting a debit will increase your assets and decrease your liabilities.

FA – Fixed Assets are your long-term assets. That means that they will benefit the company for more than one year. This could be things such as your machinery, buildings and other equipment. Fixed assets can be sub-divided into tangible and intangible.

FE - Fixed Expenses are the costs of running your business that are fixed and do not change; for example your rent payments.

GL - General Ledger is a record of all the financial transactions of a business over the life of the company. This can also be referred to as NL or Nominal Ledger.

GAAP - Generally Accepted Accounting Principles. Is a set of rules and guidelines developed by the accounting industry for companies to follow when producing their financial information. You may also hear FRS which means the Financial Reporting Standards and also relates to a set of rules to be used when drawing up your financial statements.

GP - Gross Profit is calculated in the P&L (Profit & Loss) statement by deducting your cost of sales from your sales.

HMRC – Her majesty's revenue and customs is the tax office in the UK. Something to note is that HMRC want to revolutionise the tax system and have called this ambitious plan MTD (Making Tax Digital)

ICB – Institute of Certified Bookkeepers is a British not for profit organisation supporting bookkeepers. If you are going to use the services of an external bookkeeper I would strongly advise that you use one that is ICB or AAT qualified.

ICAEW – Institute of Charted Accountants in England and Wales is a professional training an accreditation body that supports Chartered Accountants. Like all the other accounting bodies this monitors its members to ensure the highest levels of competency.

KPI – Key Performance Indictors are used to measure your business's performance of a particular activity. For example a property investor should measure his ROI for each property on an annual basis to ensure the property is still a sound investment.

LTL – Long Term Liabilities are amounts owed by your company that are payable over more than one year for example the mortgage on your factory.

MTD – Making Tax Digital is HMRC's initiative to digitalise the tax system. This will require all businesses and individuals to maintain their records using compatible software and submit returns to HMRC digitally.

NP – Net Profit is calculated in your P&L (Profit & Loss) statement and is then carried across to your BS (Balance sheet). It is calculated by taking your GP (Gross Profit) and deducting your expenses/overheads. There are usually two amounts noted in your net profit; your PBT (Profit before tax) and POT (Profit after tax)

P&L — Profit and Loss Statement is a report used to measure the company's profit over a specific time. They can be set up differently but will cover the same general information. It will show your sales/revenue less your cost of sales = gross profit less your expenses/overheads = net profit.

PAYE – Pay As You Earn is an income tax you pay to HMRC on your wages or salaries. As a business owner it is your responsibility to deduct PAYE from your employees and pay it over to HMRC.

TB – Trial balance is a document which lists all the nominal (general) ledger accounts in the business at a particular time. The totals of the GL accounts are noted in either a debit or a credit column. The trial balance is used to ensure that the bookkeeping is done correctly, and the debit and credit columns should balance, if they don't then there is a problem.

ROI – Return on investment is used to measure the financial performance relevant to the amount of money invested. It is expressed as a percentage.

VAT — Value Added Tax is the sales tax that is payable in the UK. In some countries they have GST (General Sales Tax). The VAT law in the UK is a minefield and if there is any reason to get the best accountant and bookkeepers it would be to keep you on the right side of the VAT law.

VE - Variable Expenses are the costs of running your business that will change depending on other factors. An example of a variable expense would be your utility bills.

Other terms you may find useful.

Assets – I usually refer to these as the good tools in your business. The tools you use to make money. They are split into two categories; fixed and current. Examples are machines, stocks or inventory.

Capital Allowances – Are tax reliefs available to business that invest profits back into the business by purchasing assets to use within the business. For example, if you bought a new machine for your factory then this would qualify for a capital allowance. Be aware though, that capital allowance thresholds change regularly. So, before you purchase any assets speak to your accountant to make sure you are making the best use of these allowances.

Equity – This is what your shares in the business are valued at in total. It is calculated by taking all your assets and subtracting all your liabilities. So, if your company is highly geared then you could be in negative equity. It may also be known as Owner's Equity.

Expenses – These are the day-to-day running costs of your business and are generally split into four categories which have been listed above; FE, VE, AE, OE.

Geared / gearing – This is the ratio of debit to equity in the company and is used by financial institutions to measure the company's ability to pay its debts using its own equity.

Insolvency – This is when a company or individual can no longer meet their financial obligations when they become due.

Liabilities – These are the amounts owed by your company. They would include items like bank loans, overdrafts and creditors. There are two types of liabilities; current (CL) and long term (LTL)

R&D Relief – In my opinion this is HMRC's best kept secret. Research & Development Relief is a very generous tax relief you can claim for certain expenses. Have a chat to a R&D tax specialist to see if you qualify. One of my clients wiped out their entire tax bill with this generous relief.

If you would like to get in touch or need more help you can contact me via email at hello@chantalmatthews.com.

I have some helpful giveaways for you.

To receive yours, subscribe at www.chantalmatthews.com

If you would like to learn more about property investing and be the first to receive deals available, then you can sign up to my mailing list at: https://www.endlesspropertysolutions.co.uk

Good luck to all of you and remember "Thoughts lead to actions which lead to results." So, control your thoughts, take massive amounts of income generating action and you will see results.

Acknowledgements:

I would like to take this opportunity to thank

Gordon Allen, your encouragement has paved my way.

Thank you!

www.ingramcontent.com/pod-product-compliance
Lightning Source LLC
Chambersburg PA
CBHW061205180526
45170CB00002B/970